Sweet P

Recipes

© Copyright 2016. Laura Sommers.
All rights reserved.
No part of this book may be reproduced in any form or by any electronic or mechanical means without written permission of the author. All text, illustrations and design are the exclusive property of
Laura Sommers

Introduction	1
Sweet Potato Soup	2
Spicy Sweet Potato Soup	3
Sweet Potato Chips	5
Whole Wheat Sweet Potato Muffins	6
Chicken Sweet Potato Skillet	8
Pumpkin and Sweet Potato Soup	9
Sweet Potato and Apple Soup	11
Spicy Sweet Potato and Coconut Soup	12
Sweet Potato Casserole	14
Scalloped Sweet Potatoes and Apples	15
Kentucky Bourbon Sweet Potatoes	16
Onion Roasted Sweet Potatoes	17
Cinnamon Roasted Sweet Potatoes	18
Chipotle Sweet Potatoes	19
Sweet Potato Fusion French Fries	20
Tropical Sweet Potato Fries	21
Candied Sweet Potatoes	22
Praline Sweet Potatoes	23
Sweet Potato Souffle	24
Sweet Potato Crisp	25
Sweet Potato Sausage and Cheese Bake	26
Grilled Sweet Potatoes with BBQ Baked Beans and Cilantro Cream	28
Sweet Potato and Kale Salad	30
Sweet Potato Risotto	32

Bacon Wrapped Sweet Potato Bites	34
Turkey and Yam Spicy Tacos	35
Yam Brownies	36
Sweet Potato Smoothie	37
Sweet Potato and Apple Casserole	38
Sweet Potato and Acorn Squash Holiday Casserole	39
Sweet Potato and Pineapple Casserole	41
Island Sweet Potato Bake	42
Chinese Sweet Potato Pudding	43
Roasted Sweet Potatoes	44
Avocado Stuffed Sweet Potatoes	45
Sweet Potato Cranberry Bake	46
Sweet Potato Waffles with Cranberry Maple Syrup	47
Sweet Potato Biscuits	49
Sweet Potato Pie	50
Sweet Potato and Coconut Bread	51
Sweet Potato Bread	52
Sweet Potato, Pear and Pineapple Bread Pudding	54
Pecan Sweet Potato Bread	56
Sweet Potato Banana Bread	57
Sweet Potato Hash	58
Sweet Potato Scones	59
Sweet Potato Pancakes	61
Sweet Potato Hummus	62
Sweet Potato Crackers	63
Baked Sweet Potato Fries	65
Sweet Potato Chili	66

Curried Sweet Potato Salad 67
Balsamic Glazed Wweet Potato Pasta 68
Black Bean and Sweet Potato Burger 69
Sweet Potato Falafel 70
Whole Wheat Sweet Potato Gnocchi 71
Sweet Potato Sushi 73
Curried Lentils With Sweet Potatoes and Swiss Chard 77
Sweet Potato Quesadillas 79
Sweet Potato Chocolate Pudding 81
Sweet Potato Cake Bites 82
Sweet Potato Brownies 83
About the Author 84
Other books by Laura Sommers 85

Introduction

Sweet potatoes are not just a holiday side dish! Although they go great with your Christmas or Thanksgiving feast, they are versatile and flavorful enough to have all year round. As one of the healthiest food, they are bursting with vitamin B6, vitamin D, vitamin C, Iron, magnesium and potassium. The sweet potato is a great source of energy and help quench the sweet tooth in all of us.

Enjoy your sweet potatoes in a variety of dishes with this cookbook bursting with mouth-watering and succulent recipes. There are recipes for the main course, lunch, dinner, breakfast and dessert! This recipe book is here with tons of delicious, mouth-watering sweet potato recipes for you to make and enjoy!

Sweet Potato Soup

Ingredients:

2 sweet potatoes
2 white potatoes
1 turnip
1/2 cup heavy whipping cream
6 cups chicken broth
1 tbsp. brown sugar
1 1/2 tsps. ground nutmeg
2 tbsps. margarine or butter
Salt to taste
ground black pepper to taste

Directions:

1. Peel and cut potatoes in to small, pieces.
2. Place in a pot, and cover with the chicken stock.
3. Bring to a boil, and cook until potatoes are tender.
4. Place potatoes and liquid into a food processor and puree until smooth.
5. Return pureed potatoes to the saucepan.
6. Slowly stir in the cream, brown sugar, nutmeg, and butter. Add salt and pepper to taste.
7. Serve and enjoy!

Spicy Sweet Potato Soup

Ingredients:

1/2 cup sour cream
1 tsp. grated lime zest
2 large sweet potatoes, peeled and cubed
1 tbsp. butter
1 onion, sliced
2 cloves garlic, sliced
4 cups chicken stock
1/2 tsp. ground cumin
1/4 tsp. crushed red pepper flakes
2 tbsps. grated fresh ginger root
1/4 cup smooth peanut butter
1 lime, juiced
2 tbsps. chopped fresh cilantro
Salt to taste
1 large plum tomato, seeded and diced

Directions:

1. In a small bowl, stir together the sour cream and lime zest.
2. Set aside in the refrigerator to allow the flavors to blend.
3. Melt butter in a large pot over medium heat.
4. Add onion and garlic, and cook for about 5 minutes, until softened.
5. Add sweet potatoes, and chicken stock.
6. Season with cumin, chili flakes and ginger.
7. Bring to a boil.
8. Reduce heat to low, cover, and simmer for 15 minutes, until potatoes are tender.
9. Puree the soup in a blender.
10. Whisk peanut butter into the soup, and heat through.
11. Stir in lime juice, and salt.

12. Ladle into warm bowls, and top with a dollop of the reserved sour cream, a few pieces of diced tomato, and a sprinkle of cilantro.
13. Serve and enjoy!

Sweet Potato Chips

Ingredients:

2 tbsps. olive oil
2 tbsps. maple syrup
1/4 tsp. cayenne pepper
3 large sweet potato, peeled and cut into
1/4-inch slices salt and pepper to taste

Directions:

1. Preheat oven to 450 degrees F (230 degrees C).
2. Line a baking sheet with aluminum foil.
3. Stir together olive oil, maple syrup, and cayenne pepper in a small bowl.
4. Brush the sweet potato slices with the maple mixture and place onto the prepared baking sheet.
5. Sprinkle with salt and pepper to taste.
6. Bake for 8 minutes, then turn the potato slices over, brush with any remaining maple mixture, and continue baking until tender in the middle, and crispy on the edges, about 7 more minutes.
7. Serve and enjoy!

Whole Wheat Sweet Potato Muffins

Ingredients:

1 sweet potato
2 cups whole wheat flour
1 tsp. baking soda
1/2 tsp. salt
1 tsp. ground cinnamon
1/4 tsp. ground nutmeg
1/4 tsp. ground ginger
1/4 tsp. ground cloves
1/4 cup vegetable oil
2 eggs, lightly beaten
1 tsp. vanilla extract
1 cup honey
1 (6 oz.) container vanilla yogurt
1/2 cup oatmeal
1/2 cup brown sugar
1/2 cup almonds
1 tsp. cinnamon

Directions:

1. Preheat an oven to 400 degrees F (200 degrees C).
2. Grease 16 muffin cups, or line with paper muffin liners and set aside.
3. Stab sweet potato several times with a fork and place onto a baking sheet.
4. Bake the sweet until easily pierced with a fork, about 40 minutes.
5. When the potato is cool enough to handle, peel and mash.
6. Reduce the oven temperature to 350 degrees F (175 degrees C).
7. Whisk together the flour, baking soda, salt, the 1 tsp. cinnamon, nutmeg, ginger, and cloves.

8. Stir in the vegetable oil, eggs, vanilla, honey, yogurt, and mashed sweet potato, just until all ingredients are moistened.
9. Spoon batter evenly into prepared muffin cups.
10. Blend together the oatmeal, brown sugar, almonds, and the remaining 1 tsp. cinnamon in a blender.
11. Sprinkle topping over unbaked muffins.
12. Bake muffins until golden and the tops spring back when lightly pressed, 12 to 15 minutes.
13. Serve and enjoy!

Chicken Sweet Potato Skillet

Ingredients:

1 tbsp. olive oil, or as needed
1 skinless, boneless chicken breast half, cut into cubes
1 large sweet potato, peeled and cut into 1/2-inch pieces
1 tbsp. Irish whiskey
1 tbsp. minced fresh sage
1 pear - peeled, cored, and cut into 1/2-inch pieces
1/2 cup water
2 cups baby spinach
1/4 cup chopped toasted hazelnuts
Salt and ground black pepper to taste

Directions:

1. Heat olive oil in a skillet over medium heat; cook and stir chicken in the hot oil until browned, 3 to 5 minutes.
2. Remove chicken with a slotted spoon and place on a plate.
3. Cook and stir sweet potato in the same skillet over medium heat until slightly browned, 5 to 10 minutes; return chicken to the skillet. Add whiskey, sage, pear, and water; stir well. Partially cover skillet, lower heat to medium-low, and cook until chicken is no longer pink in the center and sweet potato is tender, about 10 minutes.
4. Remove lid and sprinkle spinach over the chicken-sweet potato mixture; cook, stirring occasionally, until spinach is wilted, about 5 minutes.
5. Stir in hazelnuts; season with salt and black pepper.
6. Serve and enjoy!

Pumpkin and Sweet Potato Soup

Ingredients:

1 tbsp. coriander seeds
2 tsps. cumin seeds
2 tsps. dried oregano
1 tbsp. fennel seeds
1/2 tsp. crushed red pepper
1/2 tsp. salt
1/2 tsp. whole black peppercorns
1 clove garlic
2 tbsps. olive oil, divided
1 medium sugar pumpkin
4 orange-fleshed sweet potatoes
1 large onion, chopped
1 1/2 quarts chicken broth

Directions:

1. Preheat oven to 400 degrees F (200 degrees C).
2. In a mortar or spice grinder, grind coriander, cumin, oregano, fennel, red pepper, salt and peppercorns into a coarse powder. Blend in garlic and 1 tbsp. olive oil to form a paste.
3. Wash pumpkin, and cut into 2-inch wide wedges, scraping away seeds. Peel potatoes and cut each potato lengthwise into 6 wedges
4. Smear the pumpkin and the potatoes with the spice paste and place in a baking dish.
5. Roast 30 to 40 minutes, until tender and just beginning to blacken at the thinnest points.
6. In a large pot over medium heat, cook the onion in the remaining 1 tbsp. olive oil until translucent.
7. Chop pumpkin and potatoes into smaller chunks and puree in a blender with some of the chicken broth until smooth.

8. Be sure to scrape the roasted spice paste off the baking dish and include it in the puree.
9. Pour the pureed vegetables into the pot with the onions, and stir in as much additional chicken stock as needed to achieve the desired consistency.
10. Heat through.
11. Serve and enjoy!

Sweet Potato and Apple Soup

Ingredients:

2 (1 lb.) sweet potatoes, quartered
1 large tart apple, peeled and cored
2 tbsps. olive oil
1 onion, chopped
2 stalks celery, chopped
1 large carrot, chopped
1 bay leaf
5 cups chicken broth
1 cup cream
1 lemon, zested and juiced
Salt and pepper to taste
1 cup crumbled goat cheese or feta cheese

Directions:

1. Preheat the oven to 400 degrees F (200 degrees C).
2. Place the sweet potatoes and apple on a greased baking sheet, and roast for about 40 minutes in the preheated oven, or until tender.
3. Cool, and peel sweet potatoes.
4. Heat olive oil in a soup pot over medium heat.
5. Add the onion, celery, bay leaf, and carrot; sauté until tender. Remove the bay leaf, and discard.
6. Add the chicken broth, sweet potato and apple.
7. Puree until smooth.
8. Return to the pot, and stir in the cream, lemon zest, and lemon juice.
9. Season with salt and pepper as needed.
10. Heat through, but do not boil.
11. Ladle into serving bowls, and garnish with crumbled cheese.
12. Serve and enjoy!

Spicy Sweet Potato and Coconut Soup

Ingredients:

1 1/2 lbs. sweet potatoes
1 tbsp. vegetable oil
1 onion, chopped
1 (2 inch) piece fresh ginger root, thinly sliced
1 tbsp. red curry paste
1 (15 oz.) can unsweetened coconut milk
3 cups vegetable broth
3 1/2 tbsps. lemon juice
1 tsp. sea salt
1 tbsp. toasted sesame oil
1/2 cup fresh cilantro, chopped

Directions:

1. Preheat the oven to 400 degrees F (200 degrees C).
2. Place the sweet potatoes directly on the rack and bake until tender enough to easily pierce with a fork, about 45 minutes.
3. Remove from the oven and allow to cool.
4. Heat the oil in a large saucepan or soup pot over medium heat. Add the onion and ginger; cook and stir until tender, about 5 minutes. Stir in the curry paste and heat for 1 minute, then whisk in the coconut milk and vegetable broth.
5. Bring to a boil, then reduce heat to low and simmer for about 5 minutes.
6. Remove the skins from the sweet potatoes and cut into bite size chunks. Add to the soup and cook for 5 more minutes so they can soak up the flavor. Stir in lemon juice and season with salt.
7. Ladle into bowls and garnish with a drizzle of sesame oil and a little bit of cilantro.

8. Serve and enjoy!

Sweet Potato Casserole

Ingredients:

4 cups sweet potato, cubed
1/2 cup white sugar
2 eggs, beaten
1/2 tsp. salt
4 tbsps. butter, softened
1/2 cup milk
1/2 tsp. vanilla extract
1/2 cup packed brown sugar
1/3 cup all-purpose flour
3 tbsps. butter, softened
1/2 cup chopped pecans

Directions:

1. Preheat oven to 325 degrees F (165 degrees C).
2. Put sweet potatoes in a medium saucepan with water to cover. Cook over medium high heat until tender; drain and mash.
3. In a large bowl, mix together the sweet potatoes, white sugar, eggs, salt, butter, milk and vanilla extract. Mix until smooth. Transfer to a 9x13 inch baking dish.
4. In medium bowl, mix the brown sugar and flour.
5. Cut in the butter until the mixture is coarse. Stir in the pecans. Sprinkle the mixture over the sweet potato mixture.
6. Bake in the preheated oven 30 minutes, or until the topping is lightly brown.
7. Serve and enjoy!

Scalloped Sweet Potatoes and Apples

Ingredients:

6 sweet potatoes
1 1/2 cups apples, peeled, cored and sliced
1/2 cup brown sugar
1/2 tsp. salt
1 tsp. ground mace
1/4 cup butter

Directions:

1. Place sweet potatoes in a large pot with enough water to cover, and bring to a boil.
2. Boil until tender, then cool, peel, and cut into 1/4 inch slices.
3. Preheat oven to 350 degrees F (175 degrees C).
4. Grease a 9x13 inch baking dish.
5. Arrange half the sweet potatoes in the bottom of the prepared baking dish. Layer half of the apples over the sweet potatoes.
6. In a small bowl, mix together brown sugar, salt, and mace, then sprinkle half of the mixture over the apple layer.
7. Dot with half the butter.
8. Repeat layers of sweet potato and apple, and top with remaining brown sugar mixture and butter.
9. Bake for 50 minutes, until apples are tender and top is golden brown.
10. Serve and enjoy!

Kentucky Bourbon Sweet Potatoes

Ingredients:

6 large sweet potatoes, peeled and sliced
1 cup white sugar
1/2 cup butter
1/2 cup bourbon
1/2 tsp. vanilla extract

Directions:

1. Preheat oven to 350 degrees F (175 degrees C).
2. Arrange sweet potatoes in a 9x13 inch baking dish.
3. Combine sugar, butter, bourbon and vanilla extract in a large saucepan and heat to a boil. As soon as the sauce comes to a boil pour it over the sweet potatoes.
4. Bake 30 to 40 minutes or until the sweet potatoes are soft.
5. Serve and enjoy!

Onion Roasted Sweet Potatoes

Ingredients:

2 (1 oz.) packages dry onion soup mix
2 pounds sweet potatoes, peeled and diced
1/3 cup vegetable oil

Directions:

1. Preheat oven to 450 degrees F (230 degrees C).
2. In a large bowl, toss the dry onion soup mix, sweet potatoes and vegetable oil until the sweet potatoes are well coated.
3. Arrange the mixture on a large baking sheet.
4. Bake in the preheated oven 40 to 50 minutes, or until the sweet potatoes are tender.
5. Serve and enjoy!

Cinnamon Roasted Sweet Potatoes

Ingredients:

1/4 cup vegetable oil
2 lbs. sweet potatoes, peeled and sliced
2 tbsps. brown sugar
1 tsp. ground cinnamon
3/4 tsp. salt 1 pinch freshly ground pepper
1 tbsp. lime juice (optional)

Directions:

1. Preheat the oven to 375 degrees F (190 degrees C).
2. Pour the oil into a 9x13 inch baking dish, and place in the oven until hot, about 5 minutes.
3. Add potatoes to the oiled dish, and bake for 20 minutes in the preheated oven, turning after 10 minutes. In a small bowl, mix together the brown sugar, cinnamon, salt, and pepper.
4. After the 20 minutes is up, remove the potatoes from the oven, and sprinkle with the brown sugar mixture.
5. Stir to coat.
6. Return to the oven, and roast for another 10 minutes, or until potatoes are tender and golden brown.
7. Stir potatoes as necessary to allow them to brown evenly.
8. Remove potatoes to paper towels to drain.
9. Transfer to a serving dish.
10. Sprinkle with lime juice.
11. Serve and enjoy!

Chipotle Sweet Potatoes

Ingredients:

6 sweet potatoes, peeled and quartered
5 tbsps. butter, melted
3 tbsps. brown sugar, or more to taste
1 tbsp. onion powder
1 tbsp. garlic powder
1 tbsp. chipotle chile powder, or more to taste
1 1/2 tsps. salt
1 tsp. ground black pepper

Directions:

1. Preheat oven to 400 degrees F (200 degrees C).
2. Line a baking sheet with parchment paper.
3. Toss sweet potatoes and butter together in a large bowl.
4. Whisk brown sugar, onion powder, garlic powder, chipotle chile powder, salt, and black pepper together in a small bowl; sprinkle over sweet potatoes and toss to coat.
5. Pour potatoes in a single layer onto the prepared baking sheet.
6. Roast in the preheated oven until potatoes are tender, 30 to 45 minutes.
7. Serve and enjoy!

Sweet Potato Fusion French Fries

Ingredients:

2 sweet potatoes, cut into French fries 1 tbsp. olive oil 1/4 cup Parmesan cheese 2 tbsps. chopped fresh cilantro
sea salt and ground black pepper to taste

Directions:

1. Preheat oven to 425 degrees F (220 degrees C).
2. Combine sweet potatoes and olive oil together in a bowl; toss to coat potatoes completely. Spread sweet potatoes in an even layer on a baking sheet.
3. Bake fries in the preheated oven, turning once, until cooked through and crisp, 20 to 25 minutes.
4. Transfer fries to a bowl and sprinkle Parmesan cheese and cilantro over the top; toss to coat.
5. Season with sea salt and pepper to taste.
6. Serve and enjoy!

Tropical Sweet Potato Fries

Ingredients:

2 sweet potatoes, unpeeled
2 tbsps. olive oil, or as needed
Salt and ground black pepper
1 tbsp. sea salt
1 1/2 tsps. grated lime zest
1/8 tsp. chili powder
1/8 tsp. paprika
1/8 tsp. crushed red pepper flakes
1/4 cup chopped fresh cilantro

Directions:

1. Place the sweet potatoes into a large pot and cover with water. Bring to a boil over high heat, then reduce heat to medium-low, cover, and simmer until tender, about 20 minutes.
2. Drain and allow to steam dry for a minute or two.
3. Allow to cool, then slice each sweet potato into wedges. Arrange wedges on a baking sheet.
4. Preheat an oven to 400 degrees F (200 degrees C).
5. Brush the sweet potato wedges with olive oil, and lightly season with salt and pepper.
6. Combine sea salt, lime zest, chili powder, paprika, and crushed red pepper flakes in a small bowl.
7. Bake in the preheated oven until golden brown on all sides, about 20 minutes.
8. Plate and sprinkle with the seasoning mixture and cilantro immediately.
9. Serve and enjoy!

Candied Sweet Potatoes

Ingredients:

4 pounds sweet potatoes, quartered 1
1/4 cups margarine
1 1/4 cups brown sugar
3 cups miniature marshmallows, divided
ground cinnamon to taste
ground nutmeg to taste

Directions:

1. Preheat oven to 400 degrees F (200 degrees C).
2. Grease a 9x13 inch baking dish.
3. Bring a large pot of water to a boil.
4. Add potatoes and boil until slightly underdone, about 15 minutes.
5. Drain, cool and peel.
6. In a large saucepan over medium heat, combine margarine, brown sugar, 2 cups marshmallows, cinnamon and nutmeg. Cook, stirring occasionally, until marshmallows are melted.
7. Stir potatoes into marshmallow sauce.
8. While stirring mash about half of the potatoes, and break the others into bite-sized chunks.
9. Transfer to prepared dish.
10. Bake in preheated oven for 15 minutes.
11. Remove from oven and cover top evenly with remaining marshmallows. Return to oven and bake until marshmallows are golden brown.
12. Serve and enjoy!

Praline Sweet Potatoes

Ingredients:

4 cups mashed sweet potatoes
1/2 cup white sugar
2 tbsps. vanilla extract
4 eggs, beaten
1/2 pint heavy cream
1/4 pound butter
1 cup packed brown sugar
1/2 cup all-purpose flour
1 1/4 cups chopped pecans

Directions:

1. Butter one 2 quart casserole dish.
2. Preheat oven to 350 degrees F (175 degrees C).
3. In a mixing bowl, combine the sweet potatoes, sugar, vanilla extract, eggs and cream.
4. Blend well, and spread evenly in casserole dish.
5. Prepare the topping by combining the butter, brown sugar, flour and pecans. Mix until crumbly, and sprinkle over sweet potato mixture.
6. Bake for 30 minutes.
7. Serve and enjoy!

Sweet Potato Souffle

Ingredients:

3 cups mashed sweet potatoes
2 eggs, beaten
1/2 tsp. salt
1 cup white sugar
1 tsp. vanilla extract
1/2 cup milk
2/3 cup margarine, melted
1 cup packed dark brown sugar
1/3 cup all-purpose flour
1 cup chopped pecans
1 cup shredded coconut
1/3 cup margarine

Directions:

1. Preheat oven to 325 degrees F (165 degrees C).
2. In a mixing bowl, combine mashed sweet potatoes, eggs, salt, sugar, vanilla, milk and margarine.
3. Blend until smooth and pour into 9x13 inch baking dish.
4. Prepare the topping by mixing together the brown sugar, flour, pecans, coconut and melted margarine.
5. Sprinkle mixture over potatoes. Bake for 30 minutes.
6. Serve and enjoy!

Sweet Potato Crisp

Ingredients:

3 cups mashed cooked sweet potatoes
1 tsp. vanilla extract
1 cup packed light brown sugar
1 cup coarsely chopped pecans
1/2 cup all-purpose flour
2 1/2 tbsps. melted butter

Directions:

1. Preheat the oven to 350 degrees F (175 degrees C).
2. Butter a 9 inch square baking dish.
3. In a medium bowl, mix together the sweet potatoes, white sugar, eggs, 2 1/2 tbsps. melted butter, milk, salt and vanilla until well blended. Spread evenly in the prepared baking dish.
4. In a separate bowl, stir together the light brown sugar, pecans and flour.
5. Stir in remaining 2 1/2 tbsps. of butter to make the crumb topping.
6. Spread topping over the sweet potatoes.
7. Bake for 25 to 30 minutes in the preheated oven, until topping is browned and crispy.
8. Serve and enjoy!

Sweet Potato Sausage and Cheese Bake

Ingredients:

2 tsps. olive oil
2 medium sweet potatoes, peeled and cubed
16 oz. Italian sausage links, cut into small rounds
2 cups kale leaves, finely chopped
3/4 cup milk
1/4 cup flour
2 cups chicken broth
3/4 cup Gruyere cheese, shredded

Directions:

1. Preheat the oven to 350 degrees F.
2. Line a 9-inch square baking dish with foil.
3. Grease the foil and set aside.
4. Heat the olive oil in a large pan over high heat.
5. Add the sweet potatoes and Italian sausage.
6. Stir to coat. Cook for a few minutes until starting to brown and then move everything around.
7. Repeat until the sweet potatoes and sausage both have golden brown exteriors.
8. In a bowl, combine the sweet potato and sausage mixture with the kale.
9. Transfer to the lined baking dish.
10. Bring a 1/2 cup milk to a low boil and then lower the heat to simmer.
11. Whisk in the flour and remaining 1/4 cup milk to form a thick paste. Add the broth, whisking to keep the sauce smooth.
12. Add 1/4 cup Gruyere and stir until melted.
13. Pour the sauce over the sweet potatoes, kale and sausage in the baking dish. Top with remaining 1/2 cup cheese and

bake for 10 minutes or until the sauce is bubbly and the cheese is melted.
14. Serve and enjoy!

Grilled Sweet Potatoes with BBQ Baked Beans and Cilantro Cream

Ingredients:

2 large sweet potatoes
2 tbsps. sunflower seed oil
1 red onion, diced
2 cloves garlic, minced
1 (15 oz.) can black beans, drained
1 cup barbeque sauce
6 oz. plain yogurt
2 tbsps. shallots, minced
1/4 tsp. salt
1 tbsp. lemon juice
1/2 cup cilantro leaves, plus more for garnish

Directions:

1. Preheat the grill to medium heat.
2. Wrap the sweet potatoes in foil individually so they are completely covered.
3. Place them onto the grill, cover and cook for 45 minutes to 1 hour.
4. Once the sweet potatoes feel very soft inside the foil, they are done.
5. When they are done, remove them from the grill and keep them in the foil until ready to assemble and serve.
6. Make the beans while the potatoes are baking.
7. Heat oil in a medium-sized pan over medium heat. Add the onions and cook for 7 to 10 minutes until soft and starting to brown. Add the garlic and cook for another 2 minutes. Then add the beans and BBQ sauce. Stir to combine the ingredients, bring the heat to low and continue cooking for another couple of minutes to heat all of the ingredients.
8. Make the cilantro cream. Place the yogurt, shallots, salt and lemon juice into a food processor and pulse several times

until smooth. Add in the cilantro leaves and pulse a couple of times just until they are chopped and incorporated.
9. Assemble the potatoes. Cut a slit down the center lengthwise of the potato and gently pull the sides apart just enough to create a well for the beans. Then add a couple spoonfuls of the BBQ beans and finish with a drizzle of the cilantro cream. Garnish with some roughly chopped cilantro leaves.
10. Serve and enjoy!

Sweet Potato and Kale Salad

Ingredients:

1 pound sweet potatoes
4 tsps. olive oil
1/2 tsp. smoked paprika Salt and pepper to taste
1 bunch lacinato (Tuscan) kale, trimmed
1 Honeycrisp apple
Dressing:
1/3 cup sesame tahini
1/3 cup lemon juice
3 tbsps. water
1 tbsp. mellow white miso paste
1 tbsp. minced shallot
1/2 small clove garlic, minced Salt and pepper to taste
1 sheet aluminum foil

Directions:

1. Position a rack in the center of the oven and preheat to 375 degrees F.
2. Line a baking sheet with Reynolds Wrap(R) Aluminum Foil and set aside.
3. Peel and dice the sweet potato into 3/4-inch pieces. Add the sweet potatoes to the prepared baking sheet and sprinkle with the olive oil, paprika, salt and pepper. Toss to coat. Bake the sweet potatoes until they are golden brown and tender, 30-35 minutes.
4. In a large bowl, whisk together tahini, lemon juice, water, miso, shallots and garlic. Season with salt and pepper. The dressing should be a thick texture, similar to mayonnaise. If the dressing seems too thick, add a bit more water to thin. Set aside.
5. In a large bowl, combine kale and the dressing.
6. Massage by hand until the kale is thoroughly coated and begins to soften.

7. Core the apple and thinly slice. Add the apple slices to the kale and toss gently to combine. Transfer the kale to a serving dish and top with the warm roasted sweet potatoes.
8. Serve and enjoy!

Sweet Potato Risotto

Ingredients:

1 tbsp. all-purpose flour
1 1/2 cups uncooked Arborio rice
1 (8 oz.) sweet potato, peeled and shredded
1/2 cup chopped onion
2 tbsps. butter, softened and divided
2 tsps. snipped fresh thyme
2 cloves garlic, minced
1/4 tsp. ground black pepper
3 cups reduced-sodium chicken broth
1/2 cup dry white wine or reduced-sodium chicken broth
1/4 cup finely shredded Parmesan cheese, plus more for serving

Directions:

1. Preheat oven to 400 degrees F.
2. Add flour to a Reynolds(R) Large Oven Bag.
3. Shake. This helps prevent bag from bursting.
4. Place bag in a 13x9x2-inch baking pan.
5. Add rice, sweet potato, onion, 1 tbsp. butter, thyme, garlic, and pepper to oven bag. Turn bag several times to mix ingredients. Arrange ingredients in even layer in bag. Fold down bag opening two times to hold it open; set aside.
6. Microwave chicken broth and wine in a medium microwave-safe bowl or measuring cup for 3 minutes on high power until liquid is hot (140 degrees F). Carefully pour or ladle liquid over ingredients in bag. Carefully unfold bag opening.
7. Close bag with tie (found inside package). Cut six 1/2-inch slits in top of bag to allow steam to escape. Tuck ends of bag in pan
8. Place pan in oven, allowing room for bag to expand during cooking without touching heating elements, wall, or racks. Bag should not hang over pan.

9. Bake 25 to 30 minutes or until most of the liquid is absorbed. Let stand 5 minutes.
10. Cut open top of oven bag carefully. Remember: Always support bag with pan.
11. Spoon rice mixture into a large serving bowl. Stir in remaining 1 tbsp. butter and 1/4 cup cheese. Sprinkle with additional cheese, if desired.
12. Serve and enjoy!

Bacon Wrapped Sweet Potato Bites

Ingredients:

12 oz. bacon strips, cut into thirds crosswise
1 1/2 pounds sweet potatoes, peeled and cut in 1/2-inch cubes
1 tbsp. olive oil
1 tbsp. melted butter
1/4 tsp. ground cinnamon
1 pinch black pepper Sea salt to taste

Directions:

1. Preheat the oven to 400 degrees F.
2. Line a rimmed baking sheet with foil.
3. Set aside.
4. Wrap each sweet potato cube with a bacon slice, holding in place with a toothpick. Place on the prepared baking sheet, toothpicks facing up.
5. Combine the olive oil, melted butter, cinnamon and pepper, stirring until well mixed. Drizzle the mixture over the sweet potato bites. Sprinkle with sea salt. Loosely tent the toothpicks with damp paper towels and wrap the baking sheet with Reynolds Wrap(R) Aluminum Foil, being careful not to pierce the foil. Bake until the potatoes are just tender, about 20 minutes.
6. Remove the foil and paper towels and return to the oven; bake until the bacon is crispy and the fat starts to render, 15-20 more minutes. Blot the excess fat with the paper towels, then serve.
7. Serve and enjoy!

Turkey and Yam Spicy Tacos

Ingredients:

1 sweet potato, peeled and diced
1 tbsp. olive oil
3/4 pound ground turkey
1 clove garlic, minced
4 jalapeno peppers, seeded and minced
1 tbsp. chili powder
1 tsp. ground cumin
1/2 tsp. Cajun seasoning
1/2 tsp. salt
1/2 cup tomatillo salsa
1/2 cup chopped fresh cilantro 16 warm flour tortillas

Directions:

1. Put the diced sweet potato in a microwave-safe bowl; cook in the microwave until cooked through and fork-tender, stirring once, 5 to 7 minutes.
2. Coat the bottom of a large skillet with olive oil and place over medium heat; cook and stir the turkey until crumbled and evenly brown, 5 to 7 minutes. Stir the onion, garlic, and jalapeno pepper into the turkey and continue cooking until the onions begin to caramelize, 7 to 10 minutes. Season with the chili powder, cumin, Cajun seasoning, and salt. Pour the salsa over everything; fold the sweet potatoes into the mixture. Allow the mixture to cook until the excess moisture evaporates. Garnish with the cilantro. Serve with the warm tortillas.
3. Serve and enjoy!

Yam Brownies

Ingredients:

1 cup butter
1 cup packed brown sugar
1 cup white sugar
4 eggs
2 tsps. vanilla extract
1 1/2 cups all-purpose flour
1 tsp. baking powder
1/2 tsp. salt
2 cups peeled and finely shredded sweet potato
1 cup confectioners' sugar
2 tbsps. butter or margarine
2 tbsps. milk

Directions:

1. Preheat the oven to 350 degrees F (175 degrees C).
2. Grease a 9x13 inch baking dish.
3. In a large bowl, cream together the butter, brown sugar, and white sugar until smooth. Beat in the eggs one at a time, then stir in the vanilla. Combine the flour, baking powder, and salt; stir into the batter just until blended. Fold in the shredded sweet potato. Spread the batter evenly in the greased baking dish.
4. Bake for 30 minutes in the preheated oven, until a toothpick inserted into the center, comes out clean. Mix together the confectioners' sugar, butter and milk until smooth. Spread over the brownies while they are still warm. They will absorb some of the glaze. Serve hot or warm.
5. Serve and enjoy!

Sweet Potato Smoothie

Ingredients:

2 medium sweet potatoes
3 cups vanilla yogurt
1 cup milk
2 cups ice cubes
1 tsp. white sugar
1 ripe banana, sliced

Directions:

1. Prick sweet potatoes with a fork, and place on a plate.
2. Cook in the microwave for 8 to 10 minutes, turning once, until tender. Cool, peel and dice.
3. Combine the sweet potatoes, yogurt, milk, ice cubes, sugar and banana in the container of a blender. Blend until smooth.
4. Serve and enjoy!

Sweet Potato and Apple Casserole

Ingredients:

4 large sweet potatoes
3 tbsps. butter
1 tbsp. cornstarch
1/2 cup packed brown sugar
1 1/2 cups apple juice
1 tbsp. lemon juice
1/2 tsp. ground cinnamon
1/2 tsp. ground allspice
3 large apples - peeled, cored and sliced

Directions:

1. Place sweet potatoes in a large saucepan with enough water to cover.
2. Bring to a boil, and cook 30 minutes, or until tender but firm. Drain, peel, and cut into 1/3 inch thick slices.
3. Preheat oven to 375 degrees F (190 degrees C).
4. Lightly grease a 9x13 inch baking dish.
5. In a small saucepan over medium heat, melt the butter with the cornstarch and brown sugar. Mix in the apple juice, lemon juice, cinnamon, and allspice.
6. Alternate layers of sweet potatoes and apples in the prepared baking dish. Pour the apple juice mixture over the layers.
7. Cover, and bake 1 hour in the preheated oven. Remove cover, and continue baking 30 minutes. Baste frequently with the juices from the pan to prevent drying.
8. Serve and enjoy!

Sweet Potato and Acorn Squash Holiday Casserole

Ingredients:

1 acorn squash, halved and seeded
1 large sweet potato, peeled and cut into 2-inch pieces
1 cup balsamic vinegar
1/2 cup apricot jam
1/4 cup pomegranate juice (optional)
1 (12 oz.) jar roasted red and yellow peppers, drained and chopped
2 tbsps. minced garlic
2 tbsps. minced fresh ginger root
1/2 tsp. Chinese five-spice powder
2 tbsps. white rice flour
1 (14 oz.) can coconut milk
1/4 cup chopped walnuts
1/4 cup pomegranate seeds
3 leaves fresh basil

Directions:

1. Preheat an oven to 400 degrees F (200 degrees C).
2. Fill a 9x13-inch baking dish with 1/2-inch of water.
3. Place the acorn squash halves cut-side-down into the dish; place the sweet potato pieces around the squash. Cover tightly with aluminum foil.
4. Bake in the preheated oven until the acorn squash and sweet potato is tender, about 45 minutes.
5. Meanwhile, combine the balsamic vinegar, apricot jam, and pomegranate juice in a saucepan. Stir in the roasted pepper, garlic, ginger, and five-spice powder. Bring to a boil over medium-high heat, then reduce heat to medium-low, and simmer until the sauce has reduced to half of its original volume, about 15 minutes. Whisk in the rice flour

and coconut milk. Return to a simmer, and cook 10 minutes longer. Keep warm.
6. When the squash is tender, drain off the water and place the sweet potatoes in a mixing bowl. Scrape the squash into the bowl, and mash with the sweet potatoes until smooth. Add the roasted pepper sauce, and continue mashing until well combined. Scrape into a serving dish, and sprinkle with chopped walnuts. Garnish with pomegranate seeds and fresh basil to serve.
7. Serve and enjoy!

Sweet Potato and Pineapple Casserole

Ingredients:

6 large sweet potatoes
2 (8 oz.) cans crushed pineapple, with juice
1/2 pound golden currants
1/2 tsp. ground cinnamon
1 2/3 cups miniature marshmallows

Directions:

1. Cook sweet potatoes in a large pot of salted water until tender, about 20 to 30 minutes. Dice the sweet potatoes and place into a 9x13 inch baking dish.
2. Preheat oven to 350 degrees F (175 degrees C).
3. Stir pineapple, currants and cinnamon into the casserole dish. Sprinkle marshmallows over the casserole.
4. Bake in a preheated 350 degrees F (175 degrees C) oven for 35 minutes.
5. Serve and enjoy!

Island Sweet Potato Bake

Ingredients:

2 1/2 pounds sweet potatoes, peeled and cubed
1 cup pineapple and orange juice blend
2 tbsps. softened butter
1/2 cup (packed) dark brown sugar
1/2 cup chopped macadamia nuts

Directions:

1. Place sweet potatoes into a large pot and cover with salted water.
2. Bring to a boil, then reduce heat to medium-low, cover, and simmer until tender, about 20 minutes. Drain and allow to steam dry for a minute or two.
3. Preheat oven to 325 degrees F (165 degrees C).
4. Return sweet potatoes to the cooking pot, and mash with juice until smooth.
5. Pack mashed sweet potatoes into a 3 quart casserole dish, dot with butter, then sprinkle with brown sugar and nuts. Loosely cover with aluminum foil.
6. Bake in preheated oven until hot and bubbly, 35 to 40 minutes.
7. Serve and enjoy!

Chinese Sweet Potato Pudding

Ingredients:

1 pound sweet potatoes, peeled and cubed
2 cups white sugar
2 tbsps. vegetable oil

Directions:

1. Place a metal steamer insert into a saucepan and fill with water to just below the bottom of the steamer. Cover, bring the water to a boil, and add the sweet potato cubes. Cover, and steam until very tender, about 30 minutes.
2. Place the steamed sweet potato cubes into a bowl, and mash them with the sugar and vegetable oil until very smooth.
3. Clean the steamer insert, and line with parchment paper. Place the mashed sweet potato pudding into the steamer over a saucepan of water as before; bring to a boil, cover, and steam for 30 minutes. Serve hot.
4. Serve and enjoy!

Roasted Sweet Potatoes

Ingredients:

1 large sweet potato, peeled and cut into 1/4 inch thick slices
1 tsp. kosher salt
1 tsp. freshly ground black pepper
2 tbsps. olive oil

Directions:

1. Preheat the oven to 350 degrees F (175 degrees C).
2. Line a baking sheet or shallow baking dish with aluminum foil.
3. Arrange slices of potato in the prepared pan so they are overlapping slightly. Season with salt and pepper and then drizzle olive oil over them as evenly as possible.
4. Bake in the preheated oven until potatoes are tender and have begun to wrinkle around the edges, about 30 minutes.
5. Serve and enjoy!

Avocado Stuffed Sweet Potatoes

Ingredients:

4 (8 oz.) sweet potatoes
1 medium red bell pepper, seeded and diced
2 avocados - peeled, pitted, and mashed
1/4 cup chopped fresh cilantro
1/4 cup olive oil
2 green onions, sliced
1/2 tsp. ground cumin
3 tbsps. lime juice salt and ground black pepper to taste
1 cup shredded Cheddar cheese

Directions:

1. Preheat the oven to 350 degrees F (175 degrees C).
2. Place sweet potatoes on a baking sheet.
3. Bake sweet potatoes for 40 minutes, or until tender, turning occasionally. Set aside.
4. In a medium bowl, mix together the red pepper, avocado, cilantro, olive oil, green onions, cumin and lime juice.
5. Cut sweet potatoes in half lengthwise, and fluff the centers with a fork. Top with the avocado stuffing. Season with salt and pepper, and top with shredded Cheddar cheese.
6. Serve and enjoy!

Sweet Potato Cranberry Bake

Ingredients:

1 (12 oz.) package whole cranberries
1 small unpeeled orange, sliced
1 1/3 cups white sugar
1/2 cup pecan pieces
1/4 cup orange juice
3/4 tsp. ground cinnamon
1/4 tsp. ground nutmeg 1/8 tsp. ground mace 1 (40 oz.) can cut sweet potatoes, drained

Directions:

1. Preheat oven to 375 degrees F (190 degrees C).
2. Combine cranberries, orange slices, sugar, pecans, orange juice, cinnamon, nutmeg, and mace in a 2-quart baking dish.
3. Bake in preheated oven until cranberries soften, about 30 minutes.
4. Stir sweet potatoes into cranberry mixture and continue baking until heated through, about 15 minutes more.
5. Serve and enjoy!

Sweet Potato Waffles with Cranberry Maple Syrup

Ingredients:

1 1/2 cups sweet potato puree
2/3 cup milk
1 egg, lightly beaten
2 tbsps. melted butter
1 1/2 cups all-purpose flour
2 tbsps. brown sugar
1 1/2 tbsps. baking powder
1 tsp. ground cinnamon
1/4 tsp. ground nutmeg
1/4 tsp. ground ginger
1/8 tsp. ground cloves
1/8 tsp. salt
Syrup:
1 cup maple syrup
1/2 cup cranberry sauce
1/2 tsp. ground cinnamon

Directions:

1. Preheat a waffle iron according to manufacturer's instructions.
2. Stir sweet potato, milk, egg, and butter together in a bowl.
3. Whisk flour, brown sugar, baking powder, 1 tsp. cinnamon, nutmeg, ginger, cloves, and salt together in a separate large bowl. Add potato mixture to flour mixture; stir until batter is just combined.
4. Ladle batter into the preheated waffle iron and cook until waffles are golden and crisp, about 3 minutes.
5. Stir maple syrup, cranberry sauce, and 1/2 tsp. cinnamon together in a saucepan over medium heat. Cook, stirring occasionally, until well-combined and heated through, 5 to 10 minutes. Pour syrup over cooked waffles.

6. Serve and enjoy!

Sweet Potato Biscuits

Ingredients:

1 cup all-purpose flour
3 tsps. baking powder
2 tsps. white sugar
1 tsp. salt
2 tbsps. shortening
3/4 cup mashed sweet potatoes
1/4 cup milk

Directions:

1. Preheat the oven to 400 degrees F (200 degrees C).
2. In a medium bowl, stir together the flour, baking powder, sugar and salt. Cut in the shortening until pieces of shortening are pea-sized or smaller. Mix in the sweet potatoes, and enough of the milk to make a soft dough.
3. Turn dough out onto a floured surface, and roll or pat out to 1/2 inch thickness. Cut into circles using a biscuit cutter or a drinking glass. Place biscuits 1 inch apart onto a greased baking sheet.
4. Bake for 12 to 15 minutes in the preheated oven, or until golden brown.
5. Serve and enjoy!

Sweet Potato Pie

Ingredients:

1 (9 inch) pie shell
1 (16 oz.) can mashed sweet potatoes
3/4 cup milk
3/4 cup packed brown sugar
1/2 cup light corn syrup
2 eggs
1 tbsp. butter, melted
1/2 tsp. salt
1/2 tsp. ground cinnamon
1 pinch ground nutmeg

Directions:

1. Preheat oven to 400 degrees F (200 degrees C).
2. In a large mixing bowl combine sweet potatoes, milk, sugar, corn syrup, eggs, butter or margarine, salt, cinnamon, and nutmeg. Blend with mixer or hand-held beaters until smooth. Pour mixture into pie shell.
3. Place in preheated oven and bake for 10 minutes. Reduce oven temperature to 350 degrees F (175 degrees C) and bake for an additional 35 minutes, or until knife inserted in center comes out clean. May have to shield crust edges with foil for last 20 minutes to prevent burning.
4. Serve and enjoy!

Sweet Potato and Coconut Bread

Ingredients:

3 cups all-purpose flour
2 tsps. baking powder
1 tsp. baking soda
1 tsp. freshly ground cinnamon
1/2 tsp. freshly ground nutmeg
1/4 tsp. salt
1 cup softened butter
2 cups white sugar
4 eggs
2 2/3 cups cooked mashed sweet potatoes
1 tsp. vanilla extract
1 cup flaked coconut
1 cup chopped walnuts

Directions:

1. Preheat oven to 350 degrees F (175 degrees C).
2. Grease a 10-inch tube pan.
3. Mix flour, baking powder, baking soda, cinnamon, nutmeg, and salt in a bowl.
4. Beat butter in a large bowl using an electric mixer until creamy, about 2 minutes. Gradually beat sugar into creamed butter until fully incorporated, about 3 more minutes. Add eggs, 1 at a time, beating each egg completely before add the next. Beat in sweet potato and vanilla extract until well mixed. Stir flour mixture, coconut, and walnuts into butter mixture until just combined. Pour batter into the prepared tube pan.
5. Bake in the preheated oven until a toothpick inserted into the bread comes out clean, about 1 hour 10 minutes.
6. Serve and enjoy!

Sweet Potato Bread

Ingredients:

1 sweet potato
1 1/4 cups white sugar
1/2 cup canola oil
2 eggs
1 2/3 cups sifted self-rising flour
1/2 tsp. ground cinnamon
1/2 tsp. ground nutmeg
1/3 cup water
1/2 cup chopped pecans (optional) cooking spray
1 cup brown sugar
1 tsp. butter
1/2 cup chopped pecans

Directions:

1. Preheat oven to 375 degrees F (190 degrees C).
2. Wrap sweet potato in aluminum foil.
3. Bake sweet potato in the preheated oven until easily pierced with a fork, about 1 hour. Set aside to cool.
4. Whisk white sugar and canola oil together in a bowl. Add eggs; mix well. Sift flour, cinnamon, and nutmeg into sugar mixture. Slowly whisk water into flour-sugar mixture until incorporated.
5. Peel sweet potato; mash into the batter. Fold in 1/2 cup chopped pecans.
6. Reduce oven temperature to 320 degrees F (160 degrees C). Spray a 9x5-inch loaf pan with cooking spray.
7. Pour batter into the prepared loaf pan.
8. Bake in the preheated oven until a toothpick inserted in the center of the bread comes out clean, about 1 hour.
9. Heat brown sugar and butter in a small saucepan over low heat until sugar is dissolved, about 5 minutes. Add 1/2 cup

chopped pecans and stir to combine. Remove from heat. Pour glaze over bread.
10. Serve and enjoy!

Sweet Potato, Pear and Pineapple Bread Pudding

Ingredients:

1 cup sour cream
3/4 cup whole milk
2/3 cup superfine sugar
3 eggs, beaten
1 tbsp. baking powder
1 tsp. vanilla extract
1 tsp. ground ginger
1 cup chopped canned pears
1 cup canned crushed pineapple, drained
1 (16 oz.) can sweet potatoes, drained and cut into chunks
4 cups French bread cubes
1/3 cup packed light brown sugar
1/4 cup all-purpose flour
1 tsp. freshly grated orange zest
1/4 cup unsalted butter, melted
1 cup chopped pecans

Directions:

1. Preheat the oven to 375 degrees F (190 degrees C). Butter a 1 quart casserole dish.
2. In a large bowl, whisk together the sour cream, milk, sugar, eggs, baking powder, ginger and vanilla. Stir in the pears, pineapple and sweet potatoes just to coat, then add the bread cubes and mix until evenly distributed. Pour into the prepared baking dish. Set aside.
3. In a separate bowl, stir together the brown sugar, flour and orange zest. Briefly stir in the butter and pecans. Sprinkle over the top of the bread pudding.
4. Bake for 30 minutes in the preheated oven, until evenly puffed up and browned.
5. Serve and enjoy!

Pecan Sweet Potato Bread

Ingredients:

1 cup butter, softened
2/3 cup white sugar
2/3 cup packed brown sugar
2 cups mashed sweet potatoes
1 (14 oz.) can sweetened condensed milk
4 eggs, beaten
1 tsp. ground cinnamon
1 tsp. ground nutmeg
1/2 tsp. ground ginger
1/2 tsp. ground cloves
2 cups baking mix (such as Bisquick ®)
2 tbsps. baking mix (such as Bisquick ®)
1 cup chopped pecans

Directions:

1. Preheat oven to 350 degrees F (175 degrees C).
2. Grease and flour two 9x5-inch loaf pans.
3. Beat butter, white sugar, and brown sugar together in a bowl until smooth. Stir in sweet potatoes, sweetened condensed milk, eggs, cinnamon, nutmeg, ginger, and cloves until well blended.
4. Place all the baking mix in a large bowl; stir sweet potato mixture into baking mix until batter is just blended. Fold in pecans. Divide the batter evenly between the two loaf pans.
5. Bake in the preheated oven until a knife inserted in the center of the loaves comes out clean, 60 to 70 minutes. Cool loaves in the pans for at least 5 minutes before removing to cool completely on a wire rack, at least 2 hours.
6. Serve and enjoy!

Sweet Potato Banana Bread

Ingredients:

non-stick cooking spray
1 cup white sugar
1 banana, mashed
1/2 cup fat-free plain yogurt
2 eggs
1 cup all-purpose flour 2/3 cup chickpea (garbanzo bean) flour 1 tsp. baking soda 1/2 tsp. ground cinnamon 1/4 tsp. salt
1/3 cup water 1 cup cooked and mashed sweet potatoes
1/2 cup semisweet chocolate morsels (optional) 1/4 cup chia seeds (optional)

Directions:

1. Preheat oven to 350 degrees F (175 degrees C).
2. Prepare a loaf pan with cooking spray.
3. Beat sugar, banana, and yogurt together in a large bowl until smooth. Beat 1 egg into the banana mixture until smooth before adding the second egg and beating again until smooth.
4. Mix all-purpose flour, chickpea flour, baking soda, ground cinnamon, and salt together in a separate bowl; add to the banana mixture with the water and beat until smooth and batter-like. Stir mashed sweet potatoes into the batter until smooth. Fold chocolate and chia seeds through the batter; pour into the prepared loaf pan.
5. Bake in the preheated oven until a knife inserted into the center comes out clean, about 1 hour. Cool in the pan for 10 minutes before slicing.
6. Serve and enjoy!

Sweet Potato Hash

Ingredients:

1 small sweet potato, cubed
1/2 small yellow onion, chopped
1 tbsp. extra virgin olive oil
1/4 cayenne pepper
salt & pepper
1/2 bell pepper, chopped
1/4 cup grape tomatoes, halved
1 tbsp. cilantro, chopped
1 egg

Directions:

1. In a small pan over medium heat, cook the potatoes & onions with the olive oil, cayenne pepper and salt & pepper, covered for about 5 minutes, until softened.
2. Remove lid and cook for another 2-3 minutes until browned.
3. Add remaining ingredients except for egg and cook for another 2-3 minutes, tossing everything together.
4. Make an impression with a spoon in the middle of the hash mixture and crack the egg into the hole. Cover and cook for 3 more minutes until whites are set.
5. Remove lid, garnish with extra cilantro or scallion and serve immediately.
6. Serve and enjoy!

Sweet Potato Scones

Ingredients:

1 1/2 cup almond flour
1/2 cup quinoa flour
1/2 cup arrowroot starch
1/2 cup brown rice flour
1/3 cup grape seed oil
1/3 cup maple sugar (or can use coconut sugar, date sugar, or lastly brown sugar just has less nutritional value)
3/4 cup rice milk (or milk of choice)
1 tbls fresh lemon juice
3/4 tsp xanthan gum
2 tbls baking powder
1/4 tsp salt
1/4 tsp ground cloves
1 tsp cinnamon
1/2 tsp fresh dried vanilla, or 1 tsp liquid vanilla
1/2 of 15 oz can of sweet potato puree
1/2 cup chopped pecans (optional)
1/3 cup maple syrup (for brushing on top of scones)
One baking sheet lined with parchment paper

Directions:

1. Whisk together sweet potato, rice milk and lemon juice (if using liquid vanilla add here).
2. In a separate bowl combine all flours, xanthan gum, maple sugar, baking powder, salt, cinnamon, vanilla and cloves (and pecans if choose), whisk out lumps.
3. Add the wet ingredients to the dry and combine with a wooden spoon.
4. Take a tbsp. of batter and drop on cookie sheet covered in parchment paper.
5. Place in oven for about 15 to 17 minutes (want firm texture and/or slightly browned bottoms).

6. After about 11 minutes or when tops of scones get a bit firm brush maple syrup over top and then continue to bake.
Serve and enjoy!

Sweet Potato Pancakes

Ingredients:

3/4 cup oatmeal
2 tbsps. almond milk
1/4 cup sweet potato, mashed (to mash sweet potato quickly, wash the potato, stab it with a fork, wrap in paper towel, and microwave for 6 minutes)
1 egg
2 tbsps. pecans, crushed
Cinnamon
Topping: strawberries and a drizzle of maple syrup

Directions:

1. Heat and grease griddle.
2. Mix first six ingredients.
3. Pour onto griddle and form pancake shape.
4. On Medium Low, cook slowly and then flip (use a plate if necessary) when golden brown.
5. Cook other side slowly.
6. Plate, top with fruit and syrup.
7. Serve and enjoy!

Sweet Potato Hummus

Ingredients:

1 large sweet potato, cubed
2 cups cooked chickpeas (I made mine from dried beans but feel free to use canned)
4 Tablespoons tahini
2 Tablespoons olive oil (you may need more if the hummus comes out thick)
2 garlic cloves, minced
Juice from 1/2 a lemon
1 Tablespoon cumin
1 tsp. sriracha
dash of nutmeg
dash of cinnamon
Salt/Pepper to taste

Directions:

1. Bring a large pot of water to a boil. Lower to medium low and add in the sweet potatoes. Cook until softened (about 10 to 15 minutes). Strain and let cool.
2. In a large blender or with a food processor, blend all the ingredients together until a desired consistency is reached. Taste and add more olive oil if dry, more sriracha if not spicy enough for you, or more lemon juice to bring out the flavors more.
3. Serve and enjoy!

Sweet Potato Crackers

Ingredients:

1-1/2 cups flour
2-1/2 tsps. baking powder (see note below)
1/2 tsp. salt
3 tbsps. unsalted butter
1 med. sweet potato, or 1 cup of puree
1 tsp. sugar
Coarse salt

Directions:

1. Preheat oven to 400 degrees F.
2. Cook sweet potato until softened, about 45-50 minutes.
3. Allow to cool and remove the skin.
4. Purée using a hand blender until smooth.
5. You will need 1 cup of the puree for this recipe.
6. Set the cooled sweet potato puree aside.
7. Place butter into the bottom of a mixer.
8. Sift flour, baking powder, sugar and salt together into a large bowl.
9. Using the KitchenAid Mixer's regular mixing attachment, mix the butter into the flour mixture until it becomes a coarse meal texture like this:
10. Switch your KitchenAid Mixer's regular mixing attachment to the dough hook attachment instead. Add the sweet potato puree and let it stir until it turns into one big clump like this.
11. Sweet potato crackers recipe - easy, healthy recipes for kids
12. Roll it into a ball using your hands. Divide dough into 4 pieces. For easier rolling, wrap it in wax paper and chill for 1/2 hour.
13. Sweet potato crackers recipe - easy, healthy recipes for kids
14. Turn out onto a lightly floured surface and and roll each very thin. Seriously, as thin as you can roll it. If you can use

rolling pin rings you'll be in better shape than I was – you've got to make sure it's all even so the crackers all bake evenly.
15. Sweet potato crackers recipe - easy, healthy recipes for kids
16. Cut using small cookie cutters. Here I'm using heart cookie cutters but I've also used these great mini-cookie cutters. Place on a jelly roll pan or cookie sheet lined with parchment paper.
17. Sweet potato crackers recipe - easy, healthy recipes for kids
18. You can sprinkle with salt, sesame seeds and a little cayenne, if desired. I skip it for the kid crackers.
19. Bake in a preheated 350 F oven on an ungreased parchment paper-lined jelly roll pan or cookie sheet for 10 minutes until bottoms are slightly browned.
20. Sweet potato crackers recipe - easy, healthy recipes for kids
21. Turn over and bake until they're crispy. The original recipe says 3-4 minutes more but mine are always another 8-12 or so ...maybe it's my cheap-o oven.
22. Sweet potato crackers recipe - easy, healthy recipes for kids
23. You want them to be crispy, not chewy. Just don't let them get too brown. Here's what they look like when they're done:
24. Sweet potato crackers recipe - easy, healthy recipes for kids
25. Cool on a wire rack before storing in a airtight container. Remember there aren't any preservatives in these so you should probably snack them up within a week.
26. Serve and enjoy!

Baked Sweet Potato Fries

Ingredients:

2 med. sweet potatoes, rinsed and dried
2 tbsps. vegetable oil
2 tsps. smoked paprika
1 tsp. coarse salt
1 tsp. garlic powder
1 tsp. freshly-cracked black pepper
1/2 tsp. cumin
1/4 tsp. cayenne (optional)

Directions:

1. Preheat the oven to 450 degrees F.
1. Cut the potatoes into thin fry shape strips.
2. Mix all other ingredients together in a large bowl and toss with the potatoes until they are evenly coated.
3. Transfer the potatoes to a large baking sheet covered with parchment paper, spread in a single layer.
4. Bake for 25-30 minutes, turning the fries once or twice to cook evenly.
2. Remove once the edges slightly begin to brown and fries begin to crisp.
3. Sprinkle course salt on top while they are hot.
4. Serve and enjoy!

Sweet Potato Chili

Ingredients:

2 cups sliced onion (1 large)
20 oz peeled and cubed sweet potato
2/3 cup diced zucchini
1-2 cans black beans, or another bean
28-oz can diced tomatoes
1 1/2 tbsp chili powder
1 tsp cumin
1 tsp salt
2 tsp orange zest
1 cup water or broth

Directions:

1. Sweet Potato Chili Recipe: Combine all ingredients in a big pot, and bring to a boil. Then lower and cook until the sweet potatoes are soft. The chili tastes even better the next day, after the flavors have had a chance to combine.
2. Serve and enjoy!

Curried Sweet Potato Salad

Ingredients:

1 lb sweet potatoes (about 2 medium), peeled and chopped into 1-inch pieces
1/2 cup 2% plain Greek yogurt
2 Tbsp mango chutney
1 tsp curry powder
1/4 cup raisins
1/4 cup chopped green onions, plus more for garnish
Kosher salt, to taste
toasted cashews, optional

Directions:

1. Place cubed potatoes in a medium saucepan, cover with cold water, and bring to a boil over high heat. Cook until the potatoes are tender but not mushy, about 10-15 minutes. Drain cooked potatoes.
2. While potatoes are draining, stir together the remaining ingredients in a large bowl. While the potatoes are still warm, add them to the dressing ingredients and stir gently to evenly coat the potatoes.
3. Chill in the refrigerator (preferably overnight) to allow flavors to meld.
4. Serve and enjoy!

Balsamic Glazed Wweet Potato Pasta

Ingredients:

2 sweet potatoes, scrubbed clean and chopped into 1 inch pieces
8 oz. of your favorite pasta
2 TBS olive oil
1 1/3 TBS balsamic vinegar
3 cups spinach
Salt, pepper, and parmesan shavings for topping

Directions:

1. Bring a pot of lightly salted water to a boil.
2. Add pasta and cook according to package directions.
3. Over medium heat add the olive oil to a large skillet.
4. Once it's heated add the sweet potatoes. Cook, stirring occasionally for about 10-15 minutes or until the potatoes are fork tender. Reduce heat to low and add balsamic vinegar. Cook stirring often for about 3-5 minutes or until the sweet potatoes are glazed with vinegar.
5. Once pasta is cooked strain it. Add the pasta and spinach to the skillet with the potatoes and stir well. Season to taste with salt, pepper, and parmesan cheese.
6. Serve and enjoy!

Black Bean and Sweet Potato Burger

Ingredients:

2 cups cooked or canned black beans
1 cup sweet potato, grated
1/2 cup almond butter
1/2 cup red onion, diced
1/4 cup Sicilian olives, diced
1/4 cup whole spelt flour or other flour
2 tbsps. tamari
3 cloves garlic, diced
1 tbsp. fresh ginger, grated

Directions:

1. Drain and rinse the black beans, place them in a medium bowl, and mash. Stir in the remaining ingredients.
2. Scoop 1/3 cup of batter at a time to form individual burger patties.
3. Place a cast-iron frying pan on the stove over medium heat. Add a bit of oil to the pan and place a few burger patties in the oil. Fry each burger for 7 to 10 minutes on one side, then flip them over and fry an additional 5 to 7 minutes on the other side, or until the centers of the burgers are cooked through. If they brown too quickly, just turn the heat down a bit to allow them to cook more slowly.
4. Serve hot, on their own or on burger buns with condiments of your choice.
5. Serve and enjoy!

Sweet Potato Falafel

Ingredients:

1 cup chickpea flour
1.5 tsp cumin
1.5 tsp coriander
1/2 tsp chili powder
2 garlic cloves, finely chopped
Juice of half a lemon
Dash salt and pepper
1/4 cup of water
1 baked sweet potato, mashed
Vegetables and tahini for garnish

Directions:

1. Begin by mixing together the chickpea flour, cumin, coriander, chili, salt and pepper, chopped garlic, juice of half a lemon, and 1/4 cup water until thoroughly combine and pasty.
2. Peel the baked potato, mash the insides with a fork and fold into the chickpea flour mixture until evenly combined.
3. Form the mixture into balls. This recipe will make approximately six. Put on aluminum foil, drizzle with olive oil, and bake in the oven at 375 degrees Fahrenheit for 20 minutes. Keep an eye on them, of course.
4. When they are finished cooking, they will be slightly firm throughout but soft when bitten into. Serve with vegetables and a drizzle of tahini. You can also eat them between a warm pita bread sandwich with a dollop of garlic yogurt, tomatoes, and red onions, all aside some hummus! But, for lunch, I like mine simple.
5. Serve and enjoy!

Whole Wheat Sweet Potato Gnocchi

Ingredients:

For the Gnocchi
2 pounds sweet potatoes
1 egg yolk
1 1/2 – 1 3/4 cup whole wheat pastry flour
Salt
For the Sausage and Kale
2 tbsps. olive oil
1 pound Italian chicken sausage, removed from casing
2 garlic cloves, minced
Pinch of red chili flakes
1/4 cup dry white wine
2 bunches Tuscan (lacinato) kale, stems removed and leaves chopped
Salt
1/2 cup freshly grated Parmesan, plus extra for serving

Directions:

1. Preheat the oven to 400 degrees. Using a sharp knife, poke several holes in each sweet potato. Bake them whole until tender. Depending on their size, this could take anywhere from an hour to an hour and a half. They will be soft to the touch when tender on the inside.
2. When the sweet potatoes are cooked, slice each one open immediately to release steam and let cool slightly. Scoop out the flesh and put through a potato ricer.
3. Place the riced potatoes in a non-stick skillet heated over medium heat. Cook for 10 minutes, or until some of the liquid has cooked off. Transfer to a bowl and let cool slightly.
4. When cooled slightly, add the egg yolk and a half cup of the flour. Stir to incorporate. The goal is to add as little flour as possible, so keep adding flour little by little until the

potatoes form enough of a dough that can be rolled out into gnocchi. It will still be a bit sticky.
5. Transfer the dough to a flat surface dusted with more flour. Cut the dough into four pieces. One by one, roll each out into a log about 1/2 – 3/4 inch thick. You can dust more flour on top of the potatoes to make this easier. Using a sharp knife, cut each log into pieces about an inch long. Transfer the pieces to a parchment lined or flour coated surface.
6. For the sausage and kale, heat the olive oil in a large dutch oven over medium-high heat. Add the chicken sausage, breaking it up as it cooks. Cook for a few of minutes, or until browned. Add the garlic and chili flakes, and cook for about 30 seconds. Add the white wine and scrape the browned bits off the bottom of the pan. Then, add the kale, season with salt, turn down the heat to medium, and cover. Cook for about five minutes, stirring the kale around occasionally. Remove the lid and to the kale finish wilting and the liquid mostly evaporate.
7. Cook the gnocchi in heavily salted boiling water for just a couple of minutes until they float. Transfer the cooked gnocchi to the sausage and kale mixture, reserving a bit of pasta water.
8. Add a small ladle full of pasta water and the Parmesan to the gnocchi, sausage, and kale. Cook for a minute until a light sauce forms. Serve with additional Parmesan on top.
9. Serve and enjoy!

Sweet Potato Sushi

Ingredients:

2 cups short grain brown rice *
3.5 cups water
1/2 tsp salt
1/3 cup rice wine vinegar
4 tsp granulated sugar
1/2 medium sweet potato
1/2 medium red bell pepper
2 cups baby spinach leaves
1/4 cup sesame seeds, optional
5 sheets dried nori **

Directions:

1. Sushi rice is generally a short grain Japanese rice which swells widely and becomes slightly sticky when cooked. Long grain or less starchy white rices are not suitable for sushi, and the same goes for long grain brown rice. Short grain brown rice is soft and the grains cling together when it is cooked, which closely mimics sushi rice. Of course you can use regular sushi rice if you prefer, but I like the nutty taste of healthy brown rice for this application.
2. ** Nori are thin, papery sheets of reconstituted dried seaweed that are used for the outside of the sushi wrap. Nori is quite essential in this case and there are no reasonable and easily accessible substitutions. However, it can generally be easily found at Asian food stores, some well stocked or specialty supermarkets, or online. While you're at it, make sure that you also have a bamboo mat for rolling the sushi (makisu), because I would never try without it.
3. Rinse the rice and pour it, along with the water, into a medium sized pot set over high heat. Bring the rice to a rolling boil for a minute or two before adding in the salt.

Cover the pot with a tight fitting lid and turn the heat down to minimum. Let the rice simmer and then steam for 45 minutes. DO NOT remove the lid during this time.
4. When the rice is cooked, remove it from the heat and set it aside in the pot while you ready the sweet potato and peppers. This will let the rice cool just slightly before it is "prepared".
5. The sweet potato can be cooked by whatever method you prefer, and if you happen to have a leftover pre-baked sweet potato in your fridge, well, all the better. If not, peel the sweet potato and slice it into 1/3? slabs. Put the slices in a microwave safe dish with a lid and sprinkle lightly with water. Microwave on high for 3-4 minutes until the sweet potato is fork tender but not mushy. Set the sweet potato aside to cool before cutting each slab into an evenly sized baton.
6. De-seed the red pepper slice it into much thinner (1/8 – 1/4? thick) sticks.
7. In a small saucepan or pot, heat the rice vinegar and sugar until the sugar is dissolved. Put the rice into a large, shallow dish with a flat bottom (I like to use my pasta serving bowl) and pour the vinegar mixture evenly over the rice.
8. Now comes the fun part! The two keys to what I consider "good" sushi are an adequate rolling technique and perfect rice. The rolling you will get the hang of after the first attempt, most likely, but the rice requires a bit of patience.
9. When you incorporate the sweetened vinegar into the rice, you don't want to just stir it in because each grain should be shiny and perfectly seasoned. Use a flat spatula to slice the rice top to bottom and flip it over, going straight up and down the bowl. Pause and fan the rice vigorously for a few seconds, and then repeat the slicing and flipping in the other direction from side to side. Fan again, and repeat this process until the grains are room temperature and glossy. What you're doing is bringing down the temperature and aerating the rice while ensuring that each

grain is seasoned. What you are NOT doing is clumsily stirring and smooshing the rice into a gooey mass.

10. Lay down your bamboo sushi mat and lay a piece of nori on top with the rough side facing up. When you first lay down the nori, you want your hands to be dry. However, as soon as you start working with the sticky rice, you want them wet. It helps to have a finger bowl an towel handy.
11. Moisten your hands thoroughly and grab a large handful of the brown rice, between 3/4 – 1 cup. Gather it into a sticky ball and use your index finger to make a well in the center. Place the rice with the hollow side down on the nori and pat it out evenly. It sometimes helps to use the smooth side of a wet spoon to do this, but that's up to you. Smooth the rice out until it is even on each edge with a 1/2? border, with the exception of the top where you'll leave a scant 1? of plain nori.
12. If the rice-free strip of nori is considered 'the top', then start assembling about 3/4 of the way down to the bottom. Spread a strip of spinach leaves down first (about 1/2 cup) and in the center of that lay your sweet potato and red pepper. If you're using sesame seeds, sprinkle a scant tbsp. in a strip just beyond the edge of the spinach so they are closer to the center.
13. Moisten the naked nori edge with a little bit of water which will help the edges to adhere when rolled.
14. Starting at the bottom end, use your fingers to hold the filling in and grab the bottom of the mat. Roll it almost all of the way over to form a roll until you have a tube with only the naked nori end exposed. Squeeze and pat the roll into a tight round shape. Use both hands to do this, even though you only see one of my chubby paws in the picture below…that's only because the other hand is holding a camera, guys.
15. Loosen the mat and continue rolling the sushi so that the moist nori contacts the rest of the roll and 'glues' itself on.
16. Repeat the process until you have five rolls.

17. Slice the sushi crosswise into little maki units using a sharp, thin blade and wiping it down with a damp cloth as it becomes sticky.
18. Serve the sweet potato sushi with a saucer of soya sauce on the side and a dollop of wasabi if you like it hot.
19. My sushi cravings have temporarily abated somewhat, albeit not entirely, and if you happen to have a fish tank in your house it would be wise to keep an eye on me next time that I'm over. Your neon tetras might start to look just a bit too much like lunch, if you know what I mean. In the mean time, however, these virtuous, nutrient rich and nuttily delicious sushi rolls are more than good enough to tide me over!
20. Serve and enjoy!

Curried Lentils With Sweet Potatoes and Swiss Chard

Ingredients:

2 tbsps. extra virgin olive oil
1 medium onion, chopped
4 garlic cloves, minced
1 1-inch piece fresh ginger root, peeled and grated
1 1/2 tsps. garam masala
1 1/2 tsps. curry powder
1 jalapeño pepper, seeded if desired, then minced
4 to 5 cups vegetable broth as needed
2 pounds orange-fleshed sweet potatoes, peeled and cut into 1/2-inch cubes (about 4 cups)
1 1/2 cups dried lentils
1 bay leaf
1 pound Swiss chard, center ribs removed, leaves thinly sliced
1 tsp. kosher salt, more to taste
1/2 tsp. ground black pepper
1/3 cup chopped fresh cilantro
Finely grated zest of 1 lime
Juice of 1/2 lime
1/3 cup finely chopped tamari almonds, for garnish (optional), available in health food stores
1/4 cup chopped scallions, for garnish.

Directions:

1. In large saucepan, heat oil over medium heat.
2. Add onion and saute until translucent, 5 to 7 minutes. Add garlic, ginger, garam masala, curry powder and jalapeno. Cook, stirring, for 1 minute.
3. Stir in 4 cups broth, sweet potatoes, lentils and bay leaf. Increase heat to high and bring to a boil; reduce heat to medium, partially cover, and simmer for 25 minutes. (If lentils seem dry, add up to 1 cup stock, as needed.) Stir in

chard and salt and pepper, and continue cooking until lentils are tender and chard is cooked, about 30 to 45 minutes total.
4. Just before serving, stir in cilantro, lime zest and juice. Spoon into a large, shallow serving dish. Garnish with almonds if desired and scallions.
5. Serve and enjoy!

Sweet Potato Quesadillas

Ingredients:

2 medium sweet potatoes
2 tsp chili powder
1 large sweet onion, sliced
garlic powder, sea salt and ground pepper to taste
4 cups baby spinach, washed and dried
1 cup shredded gruyere cheese (or mozzarella)
8 whole wheat tortillas (or rice tortillas to make this dish gluten free)
4 tsp olive oil

Directions:

1. Preheat oven to 425 degrees F.
2. Using a fork, stab the sweet potatoes multiple times, all over. Bake them on a rimmed baking dish for 45 minutes or until fork tender.
3. While that's happening, sauté your onion slices in a medium pan, on medium high heat with olive oil, salt and ground pepper to taste, for about 4-5 minutes. Set aside when done.
4. Allow the sweet potatoes to cool and then remove flesh and discard skins.
5. Combine the sweet potato flesh with the chili powder and salt.
6. Assemble your quesadilla...
7. Spread the sweet potato mixture evenly on the tortilla, about 1/4 cups worth.
8. Top with a layer of baby spinach, then onions and finally 1/4 cup cheese.
9. Cover with a tortilla and press down.
10. In a large non stick pan, heat 1 tsp olive oil. Place quesadilla in pan and warm for 3 minutes on each side, on med low heat.

11. Serve and enjoy!

Sweet Potato Chocolate Pudding

Ingredients:

1 cup well-pureed roasted sweet potato flesh (roast a large sweet potato at 400°F for 1 hour – or until super soft – peel and puree flesh in a food processor until perfectly smooth, measure 1 cup)
1/4 cup unsweetened cocoa powder
2 Tbsp pure maple syrup, preferably grade B
1/4 cup unsweetened vanilla almond milk
1/2 tsp espresso powder
1/2 tsp pure vanilla extract

Directions:

1. In a food processor, combine all ingredients and puree until well-combined and smooth.
2. Serve and enjoy!

Sweet Potato Cake Bites

Ingredients:

2 small Sweet Potatoes - steamed & mashed
½ cup Rolled Oats - grounded
¼ cup Oat Bran / Rolled Oats
¼ cup Dessicated Coconut
½ tsp. Baking Powder
¼ tsp. Salt
¼ cup Raw Walnuts - coarsely chopped
¼ cup Dried Dates - soaked in water for a few hours & coarsely chopped
¼ cup Raw Honey (I used mashed fresh dates)
2 tbsp. Olive Oil
¼ tsp. Ground Cinnamon
½ tsp. Vanilla Essence
½ tbsp. ground Flax Seed

Directions:

1. Preheat the oven at 350 degrees.
2. Greased or line baking tray
3. In a small bowl, add 1 tbsp. water with flax seed, stir and set aside for 5 minutes until the mixture thickens.
4. Meanwhile, place sweet potatoes in a steamer for 10 minutes until soft or test it by poking with a fork. Let it cool down, remove skin and mashed with fork. (You can also roast the sweet potatoes in the oven until soft. I prefer steaming because it's much easier & faster for me)
5. Add all ingredients in a bowl and mix till well-combined.
6. Shape 1 tbsp. of batter into small balls and drop onto baking tray.
7. Bake for about 12 minutes.
8. Let it cool down before keeping in air tight container.
9. Serve and enjoy!

Sweet Potato Brownies

Ingredients:

1 medium to large sweet potato
1 cup pitted dates
1/2 an avocado
1/2 cup unsweetened applesauce
2/3 cup of almond meal
1/2 cup brown rice flour
1 tsp. baking powder
1 tsp. vanilla
5 tbsp. raw cacao (or sub cocoa powder)
2 tbsp. coconut palm sugar (or sub brown sugar)
pinch of salt

Directions:

1. Preheat the oven to 350 degrees F.
2. Peel and chop the sweet potatoes into chunks.
3. Place into a pot of boiling water for about twenty minutes, until they become really soft.
4. Once they are soft strain them.
5. Next, add them to a food processor with the pitted dates and process until smooth.
6. Put all the wet ingredients into the food processor with the potato/date mix and process together.
7. Add dry ingredients and continue to process until mixture is thick and fudgy.
8. Pour into a 9x9 inch baking pan greased with coconut oil. Cook for about 25-30 minutes, until you can pierce the brownies with a fork bringing it out dry.
9. Allow them to cool for about ten minutes so brownies stick together. Remove the brownies from the tray, leaving it another few minutes before cutting them into squares.
10. Serve and enjoy!

About the Author

Laura Sommers is the Zombie Prepper Mom!

Helping you prepare for the Zombie Apocalypse! She is the #1 Best Selling Author of the "Recipes for the Zombie Apocalypse" cookbook series as well as over 40 other recipe books.

She is a loving wife and mother who lives on a small farm in Baltimore County, Maryland and has a passion for all things domestic especially when it comes to saving money. She has a profitable eBay business and is a couponing addict. Follow her tips and tricks to learn how to make delicious meals on a budget, save money or to learn the latest life hack!

Visit her Amazon Author Page to see her latest books:

amazon.com/author/laurasommers

Visit her blog for more life hacks or money saving ideas:

http://zombiepreppermom.blogspot.com/

Visit her on Facebook for up to date notices on what the Zombie Prepper Mom has cooking!

https://www.facebook.com/zombiepreppermom

Follow the Zombie Prepper Mom on Twitter:

http://www.twitter.com/zombieprepmom

Other books by Laura Sommers

- Easy to Make Party Dip Recipes: Chips and Dips and Salsa and Whips!
- Super Slimming Vegan Soup Recipes!
- Popcorn Lovers Recipe Book
- Inexpensive Low Carb Recipes
- Recipes for the Zombie Apocalypse: Cooking Meals with Shelf Stable Foods
- Best Traditional Irish Recipes for St. Patrick's Day
- Awesome Sugar Free Diabetic Pie Recipes

May all of your meals be a banquet
with good friends and good food.

Printed in Great Britain
by Amazon